Alfred Dawson

Legends of the Night

Alfred Dawson

Legends of the Night

ISBN/EAN: 9783337152819

Printed in Europe, USA, Canada, Australia, Japan

Cover: Foto ©ninafisch / pixelio.de

More available books at **www.hansebooks.com**

LEGENDS OF THE NIGHT.

BY

ALFRED DAWSON, M.A.

CHRIST COLLEGE CAMBRIDGE.

> The lights burn blue—is it not dead midnight?
> Cold fearful drops stand on my trembling flesh,
> What? do I fear myself? there's none else by.
> SHAKESPEARE

LONDON:
CHARLES J. SKEET, PUBLISHER,
10, KING WILLIAM STREET, CHARING CROSS.
1860.

LONDON:
Printed by A. Schulze, 13, Poland Street.

CONTENTS.

THE THREE TALES.

	PAGE
The Weir-Wheel.	1
The Upward Gaze.	5
The Watcher.	10
The Night Coach.	15

SONGS.

Waiting for Thee.	45
The Dream.	47
The Pardon.	48

BALLADS.

The Fragment.	80
The Bell of Beaujey.	82
Where, where art Thou?	85

LEGENDS OF THE NIGHT.

The Weir-Wheel.

A WOEFUL wight, and a weary moan;
   Merry go round the weir-wheel—
I have sate me many a year alone,
For I am the wight, and I moaned the moan—
   And 'tis woe of the merry weir-wheel.

The bells ring over the meadows gay—
   Merry go round the weir-wheel.
The hedditch is fresh beneath the hay,
The dew is cool and to-morrow's the day—
   And 'tis woe of the merry weir-wheel.

THE WEIR-WHEEL.

There's a blossom white and a garland green—
    Merry go round the weir-wheel;
A blossom white, and a garland green,
And a gentle bride is there, I ween—
    And 'tis woe of the merry weir-wheel.

The raven sate on an alder dank—
    Merry go round the weir-wheel.
And he croak'd his croak as who but he,
As he sate him alone on his alder-tree—
    And 'tis woe of the merry weir-wheel.

She wander'd there by the alder dank—
    Merry go round the weir-wheel,
Where the nenufar bright and the bulrush rank
Were clustering near the glidly bank
    To the sound of the merry weir-wheel.

To cull me a nenufar cold and bright—
    Merry go round the weir-wheel,
She lean'd her o'er in the dusky night,
And heard not the wail of the water sprite,
    In the gush of the merry weir-wheel.

THE WEIR-WHEEL.

The dusky night is past and o'er—
   Merry go round the weir-wheel;
The dusky night is past and o'er,
But that fair bride came back no more—
   And 'tis woe of the merry weir-wheel.

They sought her east, and west and east—
   Merry go round the weir-wheel,
They sought long years, at length they ceased,
For they found her not in west nor east,
   Still merry went round the weir-wheel.

Long years are past, and the flood is low,
   Where merry went round the weir-wheel.
And the wheel is broke, and waters low—
And shallow the stream where nenufars grow—
And a skeleton white mid the stalks below—
   Woe worth! woe worth the weir-wheel!

Woe worth the wheel—woe worth the stream—
   Where, long years so lonely,

A form, more pale than the pale moonbeam,
Pointed a spot where nenufars gleam,
   Marked by the night bird only.

The night bird saw that phantom pale,
   Near to the wash of the weir-wheel,
But in vain he call'd his plaintive tale,
He call'd long years without avail
   So long as went round the weir-wheel.

At last, it ceased, and the tale was known,
   And ruin'd is now the weir-wheel,
And since, I've sate me years alone,
A weary wight, and I moan the moan,
And 'tis ever "Woe worth the weir-wheel!"

The Upward Gaze.

ARD beside a dull wood—
    Go not there alone—
If ever you go to that dull wood,
    You'll know then what I mean.
There's a pool where flags are steeping—
    Go not there alone—
And the waters black are sleeping,
    Under a mantle green.

If you visit that spot so lonely—
    Go not there alone—
Go not there but only
    When the day is warm and bright.
There are sounds in the flags and the brambles—
    Go not there alone—
For him who thitherward rambles
    Under the shadow of night.

There are foul flies in the marsh—
    Go not there alone—
And the call of the toad is harsh,
And the owl with a ghastly scream.
But there's worse than the flies of night—
    Go not there alone—
Than the toad and the owl so white,
There's worse on the gloomy stream.

I was there at the close of day—
    Go not there alone—
I wander'd alone, astray,
    In the twilight damp and cool,
And I saw what had seen I never—
    Go not there alone—
I saw what unseen is ever
    Upon that mantled pool.

There was one by fortune slighted,
    Accursed and doom'd to moan,
Whose hope and whose heart were blighted,
    Once hitherward came alone.

THE UPWARD GAZE.

He had roam'd on travel weary
   To many a savage shore,
Pining in solitude dreary
   On what he must know no more.

He had done a deed, and he wander'd
   Lonely, pensive, slow,
And with eye upraised he ponder'd
   On heaven he ne'er must know.
On earth, he turned never
   But only a vacant stare,
The heaven regarding ever,
   For what he had lost was there.

All deem'd him a spirit crazed,
   To see his upturn'd view,
For ever and aye he gazed
   Into the ether blue;
And hither, by fortune slighted,
   In the twilight damp and cool,
With hope and with heart all blighted,
   He came to the dismal pool.

There were foul flies in the marsh,
    And the owl with a ghastly scream,
And the call of the toad was harsh,
    By the side of the gloomy stream.
But he heeded nor call nor scream,
    As he gazed on the distant sky,
And within the gloomy stream,
    He sate him down to die.

And of reeds a rustling skreen
    Shrouded his oozy bed—
And of weeds a covering green
    Closed over the sleeper's head.
There are sounds in the flags and brambles
    Ever and aye since then;
He may see who thitherward rambles,
    What may never I see again!

He will see, where the dark stream gushes—
    Go not there alone—
He will see in the flags and bushes
    A sight will make him quail.

For he who had done the deed,
    Is couched still there alone,
And from the dark green weed,
    Peers forth that face so pale.

There are foul flies in the marsh—
    Go not there alone—
And the call of the toad is harsh,
    And the owl with a ghastly cry;
But worse than the harsh toad calling,
    Than the owl with a ghastly cry,
Is the upward face appalling
    Still turned to the distant sky.

The Watcher.

"Why watchest thou here, thou pilgrim pale,
   Under the night so dreary?
     From yonder wold, a moaning gale
  Pierces this hawbush skreen, too frail
     To shelter one so weary!"

"Leave me, leave me this hawbush skreen
   To shelter me here so weary,
For I must watch, alone, unseen—
   I must watch, tho' the wind be keen,
     Thorough the night so dreary!"

" What watchest thou, thou pilgrim lone—
    Upon the heath uncheery,
With hawbush skreen and seat of stone—
    Listing still the cold wind's moan,
        Thorough the night so dreary !"

" Ride on, ride on, nor linger slow—
    Not longer here may'st tarry,
Ride on, and ere a league you go,
    What I do watch you'll haply know—
        Nor question more I parry !"

I left him there—alone—unseen—
    Pale—silent—and uncheery—
And still, as the wind blew keen more keen,
    I thought of the stone, and the hawbush skreen,
        That sheltered one so weary.

I pass'd a mile—I had pass'd not twain,
    Across the whispering heather—
But I heard a sound thro' trickling rain
    A sound, as links of a canker'd chain,
        All grating harsh together.

And I saw, where against the ashy sky,
  A dark thing waved and floated—
And ever it seemed, as it hung so high,
  As dancing alone to the night-winds sigh,
    A solemn dance unnoted.

And I hastened on, for I had no will
  To stay on the whispering heather,
Where that dark thing swung in the night-air chill
  And the rusty links, with discord shrill,
    Were grating all harsh together.

I wander'd since on a distant shore,
  And over the ocean foaming,
And many a year was past and o'er,
  'Ere I came back to that land once more,
    After a restless roaming.

There's a mound of earth with weeds o'ergrown
  Upon the whispering heather,
And, at less three miles but more than one,
  There's a scathed bush and a sunken stone,
    Close in a dell together.

" Oh, shepherd, tell what mound I see
    Beclad with weeds and broken?
And, over one mile but less than three,
    That sunken stone by the hawthorn tree,
        O tell what they betoken?"

" Once on that mound a gibbet stood,
    Stood long—a sight uncheery,
Where moulder'd as moulder'd the chains, and the wood
    He who had shed his father's blood
        In yonder dell so dreary.

" And underneath that sunken stone,
    He tried his crime to smother—
'Tis the murder'd one's grave—but the deed was done,
    Stranger, when we, now aged grown,
        Were babes both one and tother.

" And they say, that to rest he had no will
    Beneath the stone and the heather,
Whilst the parricide waved in the wind so chill,
    And the rusty chains with discord shrill
        Still grated all harsh together.

"And, till all was gone, a pilgrim lone
  Watched he the heath uncheery,
Listing ever the night-winds moan—
  By hawbush skreen and on seat of stone,
  Thorough the night so dreary."

The Night Coach.

TRAVELL'D through a doleful night—
I had travell'd a doleful day—
And the roof of the coach was a cheerless sight,
When I shiver'd alone in the lamp's dim light,
Along a desolate way.

Not quite alone—the driver is there
His hand on the trembling rein;
But his mood is sad, and his words are rare,
For he has seldom a word to spare,
Save for his horses twain.

The horses twain, with patient toil,
Slowly his word obey;
For they are spent with long turmoil—
And the wheels sink deep in the clinging soil
Along the desolate way.

This way, so desolate and so drear,
Is skirted to left and right
By fir-trees dark all crowded near,
Which fill his mind with secret fear,
Who passes alone at night.

And there's nought to hear from the gloom profound,
Of these fir-trees dark and grim,
But of horses twain the panting sound,
As they urge the wheel through the clinging ground,
In the flickering lamplight dim.

And thus with dull, reluctant pace,
We travel the dreary way—
And phantoms many, of direful face,
And thoughts of dole each other chace,
Thronging in close array.

And sure am I that driver sad
Bore part in these fancies vain,
As he tun'd the tune of a ballad glad,
Though seldom a tone to spare he had
Save for his horses twain.

For so strange his voice—and so wild his tone—
He sang as who sings in pain,
And the ballad glad it seem'd a moan,
As ever he tun'd and tun'd alone
One same and tedious strain.

And it seem'd as I heard that tedious sound,
And of wheels in the clinging soil,
And saw the dim lamp in the dark profound,
That I ever had toil'd on that desolate ground,
And ever more there must toil—

There was no longer a past for me,
Not even of yesterday—
And nothing of future could I see—
But only the future still to be
Upon that tedious way.

And sense is dull'd by torpor drear,
And thought is stagnant grown,
But now, at length, a change is near,
For yonder a light is sparkling clear,
Amid the gloom alone.

It is, methinks, a kindly gleam,
A herald-star of grace;
The driver he hums a livelier theme,
And lo! the jaded horses seem
To mend their lingering pace.

And well they may for 'tis the spot,
The well known change-house blest,
Where they, poor creatures, faint and hot,
At length may cease their painful trot,
And know a transient rest.

We have stopp'd at last beside a green,
And near a stable lone,
A stable had once a mansion been,
But now a ruin and half unseen
With ivy thick o'ergrown.

Dark firs, all ranged in solemn file,
By the fitful light are seen,
And in the midst that ghostly pile,
And there's ne'er another for many a mile
Around the lonely green.

With lamp of horn, the hostler there
Holds ready his horses twain,
And he busies himself with a sullen air
The traces to loose of our jaded pair,
And then to put to again.

The driver has thrown each separate rein
One hither, and one there—
And as he waits to start again,
Holds converse short, in mystic strain,
With him of the sullen air.

'Twas said " how Jim had westward been
By the last up Tally ho—
How both the parties he had seen—
How they were fly—and how he was green—
And could no business do."

'Twas said "as how the roan was lame—
How Miles had fired the black—
How some one could chaff, but was not game—
And how as soon as the down coach came,
They would send a basket back."

But now the reins are buckled neat—
And coupled the horses right—
The cloths are drawn and all complete—
And the driver firm upon his seat,
Mutters a rough "good night!"

And so again with lumb'ring sound
The coach is on its road;
And the horses o'er a firmer ground,
Beyond the fir-trees gloom profound,
Draw quicker a lightened load.

For we have left the sombre skreen
Of firs on either hand;
And now the air comes fresh and keen,
And misty wreaths are dimly seen
To steal o'er the open land.

And see the waning moon is there,
Low hung with threatening horn—
And through the dull and murky air
She sheds from the west a feeble glare
Upon the scene forlorn.

With steady pace, we roll along
Across a marshy plain—
The driver has now renewed his song,
As he presses oft with taper thong
The speed of his horses twain.

But cheery now the driver's strain,
And varied is his song;
He to my word responds again,
As he presses the speed of his horses twain
By a touch of the taper thong.

He is not as he was before
Sullen of mood and mien—
And he tells how twenty years, or more,
He has driven that wild country o'er,
And what he has sometimes seen.

"There's a place," he said, "near this here ground
They call it the dismal pool—
Where years ago a man was drown'd,
And he was sitting when he was found
Right up in the water cool.

"A 'quest was held—the case was tried—
But the 'quest could not agree
On who he was and when he died,
But the verdict brought in was suicide,
So buried he could not be.

"That is, not in the sacred ground,
So they buried him by the way;
And, two days after, he was found,
Still sitting there where he was drown'd,
Leastways 'tis so, they say.

"And since that time, there's none so bold,
Unless he were a fool,
To venture out by night I'm told,
And go alone in the dark and cold
Down to the dismal pool.

" But nobody ever came this way,
For then then there was no road;
And nobody pass'd by night or day,
And nothing was heard as I've heard say,
But the night-owl and the toad.

" I never was there," the driver said—
" And never wish to go :
I can see it from my box instead,
'Tis near that clump of trees ahead
Three hundred yards or so.

" But, when by night I drive this ground,
In the winter time you know,
And I see the lights a-dancing round,
Like fire-flies there where he was drown'd,
Don't I make the horses go?"

The driver's dismal tale was said,
And he made the horses go,

And methought I saw the fire-flies red,
Dancing near a corpse ahead,
One hundred yards or so.

We have left with joy the dank morass,
And mount a hill of sand,
And now a straggling hamlet pass,
Where cottages of meanest class
Are scattered on either hand.

The hamlet has an aspect ill,
Each hovel seems to frown;
And I feel each time a secret thrill,
As I pass each one in the night so still,
Thus scatter'd up and down.

I love the peasant's smiling nook,
And the porch and the woodbine screen,
And the gardens sloping to the brook
And all the cottage-homes that look
Upon the village-green.

But here's no garden by the brook,
Here is no village-green,
This way and that the hovels look,
And seem to slink each in its nook,
With sullen, unsocial mien.

The driver said, "That was a place
Before this road was made,
Where used to live a gipsy race,
Of savage look and dingy face,
And they drove some secret trade.

"This secret trade, you well suppose,
Was nothing but to rob;
But then, as everybody knows,
Such dangerous customers as those
Are ready for any job.

"A hardy numerous band they were,
With strong allies folks tell,
And in that ruin'd building there,
Where I change this and the other pair,
Lived one who knew them well.

"This one was quite of high degree,
And could help with purse and power,
And he had friends beyond the sea—
All joined in one same plot as he—
And his house was like a tower.

"This house, secure against alarms,
With guns and traps was fill'd.
And what was more than such like arms,
'Tis said that he, with drugs and charms,
An army could have kill'd.

"He liv'd a gloomy life long while,
And seldom abroad was seen.
And few went to that gloomy pile,
And no one lived for many a mile,
Around that lonely green.

"At last, this man for many a day
Was miss'd in the country round,
He seem'd to have vanish'd quite away,
No one had seen, and none could say
Where he might be found.

THE NIGHT COACH.

"And when they sent to look for him,
At his house on the lonely green,
The house was found in a dismal trim,
Open and void, but the master grim
Could neither be heard nor seen.

"Of dust and rubbish there was no lack,
And of broken seats and stools,
And there was a room with a furnace black,
And broken crucibles, and a pack
Of other outlandish tools.

"There was nothing stirring in hall or room,
Nothing upon the stair,
Nothing alive in that place of doom,
The very rats avoid the gloom,
And dare not harbour there.

"But they found in the court and near a shed,
Forgotten and alone,
An old grey horse but nearly dead,
Wasted with hunger gaunt and dread,
He was only hide and bone.

"And it was plain that famine dire
He had borne a week or more,
For from the shed he had stript the straw,
And was vainly stretching his meagre jaw
To reach a mouthful more.

"Not again this man was heard or seen,
Where ever he went or how,
Since then there's no one long has been
To dwell in the house on the lonely green,
And the house is a stable now.

"Some say that he for wealth and might
His soul had signed away—
And that at last, as is just and right,
The devil had come in the dead of night
To carry him off his prey.

"And I knew an old man, who at that day
As packman used to range,
And he was often heard to say—
That he one night had pass'd that way,
And had heard a something strange.

" He had heard at night a dismal cry
Now feeble and now strong,
Sometimes low and sometimes high,
Like one in terror passing by,
Who screamed as he went along.

" The gipsies left the country too,
Witherward none can say,
But one, the foremost of the crew,
For cruel crimes of deadly hue,
Was gibbetted on the way.

" And he alas with heavy moan
Did to a priest confess,
He had done a deed that ne'er was known,
And had hid beneath a certain stone
His unseen wickedness.

" And he said too, when the deed was done
A paper he had seen,
By which he knew he was the son—
The only child of the vanish'd one
Who had lived on the lonely green."

The driver tells so drear a tale,
As he drives his pair along,
In truth, as we thread this gloomy vale,
I would I had ne'er but heard the wail
Of his dull and tedious song.

For phantoms, of such spectral look
As fancy will invent,
Now people every leafy nook—
And haunt the sedges by the brook—
Lurking with foul intent.

There are tangled branches all around
And close depending o'er,
And of waters falling underground
Into an unknown depth profound
I hear the hollow roar.

And, as the foaming waters fell,
There seemed from time to time
To mingle with the gushing swell
The clang as of a silvery bell
Ringing a plaintive chime.

The driver sung his tedious strain,
And the foaming waters fell,
And still it came again, again,
We nearer draw, and I heard it plain,
The tone of a plaintive bell.

" What village bell is that I hear ?"
I begg'd the driver say,
" There is," said he, " no bell so near
Could send its voice so loud and clear
Into this hollow way.

" 'Tis of Bell brook you hear the tide,
So called because they say—
That in that stream a lady died,
And she poor thing would have been a bride
Had she lived to the morrow's day.

" Yet twas not in this gushing rill
That perished the maiden fair,
But over the meadows near a mill,
Where far away the waters still
Were spann'd by an ancient weir.

"The village smil'd with air serene,
And hope and joy was there,
And the merry bells o'er meadows green
Peal'd glad, whilst in the wave unseen
Perish'd that maiden fair.

"And so the stream Bell brook they call,
A name that suits it well,
For ever amid the rush and brawl—
Wheresoever the waters fall—
There chimes a plaintive bell."

"Now driver cease, three tales you've told
As sad as sad might be—
To hear them makes the blood run cold—
So drear each one, but this I hold,
The dreariest of the three."

———

The driver has ceas'd his dreary strain
And he sings his tedious song,

Nor to my word replies again,
But presses the pace of his horses twain
By a touch of his taper thong.

And now, methinks, a keener air
Breathes over the open vale—
And though no moon nor star is there,
I plainly see the country bare
Design'd in outline pale.

The coach rolls on—rolls on—rolls on—
Over an endless plain—
And many another mile is gone—
And I think this coach that I ride upon,
Never will stop again.

And still the restless rumbling wheel
Whirls over the frosty ground—
Till thought at last begins to reel—
And visions vague my senses steal—
And I sleep a sleep profound.

Long time I sleep, whilst wearily
A weary stage is past,
For weary stage must ended be—
And at the Inn of Eltess Lee.
The coach has stopt at last.

Here cheery fire and lights engage
And gladden awhile the sight;
And horsed once more is our equipage,
Before a long and dreary stage
That ends the voyage of night.

Now, from the lumbering motion free,
I seek the cheery light,
Within the little hostelrie—
And there are waiting travellers three
To join our voyage of night.

'Tis pleasing when o'er a wintry track
The hollow wind blows keen—
When roads are white—and skies are black—
To hear the crackling faggot crack
In such a homely scene.

Pleasing then the social strain
Of converse light and gay—
Pleasing the cordial cup to drain—
But—oh—'tis hard to part again
Upon the wintry way.

But now the pair is coupled neat—
And trimm'd afresh each light—
And from the hearth we must retreat—
And the driver, mounting to his seat,
Mutters a rough "good night!"

We leave the crackling hearth so gay
With recollection fond;
The turnpike lamp with pallid ray
Shows through a yawning gate the way
Into the gloom beyond.

We have left the Inn of Eltess Lee—
And are on the gloomy wold—
But cheery are the travellers three,
And their discourse is light and free,
In spite of gloom and cold.

And they travel again their journies o'er,
They have travell'd long time and far,
Two to the western and eastern shore;
The third a thousand miles or more
Towards the polar star.

The coach rolls on—more sharp, the air
Is whitening bush and spray—
And there's neither bend nor angle there—
And the road across a country bare
Stretches for miles away.

But still of all they've heard and seen
The travellers tales are told:
And what they've done—and where they've been—
They still recount with relish keen,
In spite of gloom or cold.

THE NIGHT COACH.

Right cheering is such bearing light—
And tales and talk so free—
But those three tales I heard to-night
Still are haunting me, in spite
Of the tales of the travellers three.

The coach rolls on—rolls on—rolls on—
We have gained the middle plain;
And now my journey is nearly done,
And glad I'll be when the coach I'm on
Shall come to a stop again.

There is upon the middle wold,
To a bridle path hard by,
A post upon a mound of mould,
Pointing as with finger cold
Into the leaden sky.

So desolate it looks and chill
Upon that mound of mould,
I feel of awe an icy thrill
To see it spectral white and still
Pointing its finger cold.

There sure must be some legend rare
About that silent post;
It has so weird an aspect there
Standing on its hillock bare
Like a new risen ghost.

I'll question not that driver more
Who sits in silent mood,
I've heard enough his legend lore,
The dismal tales he told before
Have verily chill'd my blood.

But the driver guessed my thoughts of dread,
Though silent was my tongue,
And he sideways slowly bent his head
As with a dreary smile he said :
" 'Twas there that he was hung !"

I well knew what the driver meant,
As he sideway bent his head ;
The travellers three no heeding lent,
And, on their travels still intent,
They heard not what he said.

Now many another mile is gone—
And 'tis bitter the freezing night—
And there, wherever the lamps have shone,
Each object draped in hoar frost wan
　　Starts out a spectre white.

With crystals branch and twig are set,
And gemm'd the feathery grass,
And broider'd on a ground of jet
Of tangled briars a silver net
　　Is glistening as we pass

The horses on their mettle got,
Their homeward speed renew—
And on they go with ardour hot,
And crisp the ground beneath their trot
　　Crackles and sparkles blue.

The driver is holding them down a swell,
And a backening rein he plies,
Then slacks his hold across the dell,
With skilful art to spring them well
　　Up the opposing rise.

But vainly now he slacks his rein
To shoot the hollow dell—
And the driver's skilful art is vain
Up the opposing rise again
To spring his horses well.

For now the horse (with sudden start)
On the off hand side who toil'd,
Towards the near side made a dart,
And I heard the loud beating of his heart
As he back from the hedge recoil'd.

And I saw his eye with terror bright,
And nostril panting wide,
As something through the dusky night,
More dusk in the coach lamp's fading light
He fearfully espied.

And I feel the swerving carriage rock
To this horse's sidelong rear,
Whilst the other motionless as a stock
Stricken by sympathetic shock
Trembles with panic fear.

THE NIGHT COACH.

And panic fear has seized me too,
The driver and travellers three,
As we turn to the hedge a startled view,
Expecting something strange and new
On the off road side to see.

Down from the coach we all alight,
We dare not there abide,
And by the coach-lamp's flickering light
We dimly see an object white
Near the off road side.

The driver hastes to take his stand
At the heads of the frighten'd pair—
Whilst we, the rest, with lamp in hand,
Approach the hedge, a cautious band,
To see what may be there.

And what there is may well with fright
The heart of the boldest thrill,
To see it at the dead of night
Sitting alone so ghastly white
Motionless sightless chill.

It seems a wither'd and aged one,
Blind, helpless, and forlorn—
As there he sits by night alone,
Resting upon a granite stone,
His back to the hedge of thorn.

Through tangled locks of hoary gray
Gleam dull the sightless eyes,
Be he old or young there's none may say,
For the frost, that has whiten'd bush and spray,
Has blanch'd his hair likewise.

And death has quench'd his open eye,
That looks, but nought can see—
And yet it seems, I know not why,
To kindle as it seems to spy
Myself and the travellers three.

With right arm raised above the breast
He steadily seems to view,
The fingers to his lips are press'd,
As of some secret he is possess'd,
And bids us guard it too.

Awe stricken with a sight so drear
Myself and travellers stand:
The driver now approaches near,
Whilst I, to calm the horses' fear,
Soothe them with word and hand.

And long we form surmises vain,
And vain suspicions tell—
But see the night hours quickly wane—
And we not longer can remain
Within this hollow dell.

And so we have left him stiff and cold,
As he sits by the off road side;
And ne'er since then has it been told
Hinted or guess'd by young or old,
When or how he died.

And since that time ('tis many a year)
I never have chanced to be

Upon that road so dull and drear—
And never have chanced to see or hear
Ought of those travellers three.

That driver too I saw no more—
His coach and his horses twain—
Since then the world I've wander'd o'er
But that night coach ride I rode before
I wish never to ride again.

Waiting for Thee.

I'M weary, love, thus waiting lonely,
   Through lingering days, nor hope is sent me,
     Waiting for thee!
Why in this world can one joy only,
   Why none of those by fortune lent me
   Why only that of all content me,
     Which cannot be?

I'm weary, love, yet still I wander,
   From spring and sunshine so uncheery
     Waiting for thee!
Glad sounds I love not—but I ponder
   Ever in stillness, to one weary
   Night's silent cloud is not so dreary,
     It cannot be!

It cannot be—Fate hath forbidden
    This wounded heart one hope to cherish
        Of what might be.
Deep in my soul must this be hidden,
    A thought which but with life can perish,
    Deep in my soul with life to perish,
        Known but to thee!

Wearily waiting, dreaming, waking
    Life so forlorn no more shall bind me.
        I will be free!
Free, through the confines of death breaking,
    Haste, love, tarry not long behind me,
    There may'st thou seek me, there wilt find me,
        Waiting for thee!

The Dream.

WHEN night silently is weeping
    Dewy tears o'er flower and tree,
In dull sleep, my senses steeping,
    Vanish'd one thou com'st to me.
        'Tis no dream—no empty seeming—
        Thy smile once more is mildly beaming—
        And as of yore with fond love teeming—
Thy living self again I see.

All the day unseen thou'rt waiting—
    Waiting still night's placid reign,
And with strong love unabating
    Thou'lt be with me there again.
        No—'tis a dream—an empty seeming—
        Thine eye no more with life is gleaming—
        Nor as of yore with fond love beaming—
Vanish'd one—my tears are vain.

The Pardon.

VER the voiceless billow
In a boat I darkly glide—
Stirs not a leaf of the willow
That weeps o'er the sullen tide.
The wave with silent motion,
Glides on to a distant main;
Lost in the fathomless ocean,
'Twill never come back again.

And the night wind has no sound,
As it passes along unseen—
To regions remote, profound,
Where never yet man has been.
Where the deep mysterious fountains
Are fetter'd with icy chain,
Engulf'd in snow clad mountains,
'Twill never come back again.

A flower on the ozier bed
Is wan in the twilight's gleam,
Dying, it droops its head
Over the sullen stream.
And its faded leaves are falling,
And 'tis still the same sad strain,
Life there is no recalling,
It never will bloom again.

Bloom never—its breath on the wings
Of the wind hath passed away.
So vanish all earthly things
With Time that will not stay.
Still o'er the voiceless billow
In my boat I slowly glide,
Stirs not a leaf of the willow,
That weeps o'er the sullen tide.

The moon with crescent lamp
Pales feebly over head;
And wreaths of vapour damp
Steal out from the river bed.

And through that vapour dank
Shapes all uncouth I see,
And nothing on either bank
Is what it seems to be.

Is that a scathed willow
Beside the water's brim,
Into the silent billow
That droops a shatter'd limb?
Methinks, as I near am borne
On the untiring flood,
'Tis a figure aged and worn,
And clad in a monkish hood.

Mysteriously reclining,
Its looks so thin and pale,
Night's pallid beam is shining
Athwart that phantom frail.
In the silent river
A ghostly hand it laves,
Something ever and ever
Seeking upon the waves.

And, or the vague wind only
Deceives my startled ear,
Or a voice is plaining lonely
In accents dull and drear—
The ghostly hand is feeling—
Seeking still in vain,
And the word comes faintly stealing,
" She comes not back again."

I have past that dreary sight,
That shape I would see no more—
And under the cloud of night
I have gain'd the further shore—
And o'er a desolate track
With quickening pace I tread,
Whiles gazing fearfully back
To the river's silent bed.

By fancies dread unceasing
Spurr'd on I have cross'd the plain,
And ever with speed increasing
A forest's skirt I gain,

Beneath that leafy cover,
With spirit calm'd I stray,
Where things unearthly hover
It is not good to stay.

Now along a bosky glade
With slacken'd step I pass,
Beneath the dark pine's shade,
And through the tangled grass—
But soon mid spray and stem
A welcome light I spy,
Glittering like a gem
Through a tissue of sable dye.

I have reach'd in a tranquil dell
A cottage of humble seeming,
'Tis a pious hermit's cell
From whence the light is beaming—
A holy man is there
His vesper hymn attuning,
Or wrapt in silent prayer,
With his soul and his God communing—

THE PARDON.

To the portal open stealing,
I watch that inmate lone,
The aged hermit kneeling,
And the crucifix of stone—
As I look on his pensive mien,
Recurs with inward thrill
The mystic form I had seen
By the side of the waters chill.

But nought can here appal
In that calm and pensive mien,
In the hoary locks which fall
Around that face serene,
His look in mute devotion
Is fixed on things above,
   And his upraised eye,
   I know not why,
Inspires a strong emotion
Of reverence and of love.

But now his vespers ending
He turns with aspect bland

A look upon me bending
By the threshold where I stand.
Within his humble dwelling
He kindly bids me stay,
Refreshment there to find
And rest till the morrow's day.

Soon at his modest board
A hermit's feast I share,
And many a courteous word
Sweeten'd the scanty fare.
But still, by hearth bright shining,
I recal with inward thrill
That mystic form reclining
By the side of the waters still.

My air absorb'd and dreaming
The hermit saw with pain,
And he cried, "'This pensive seeming,
My son, I pray explain?
Say whence the secret fear
That kindles at whiles thine eye?

And the pallor thy features wear?
I pray thee, my son, reply."

" Good father," I replied—
" I have seen a woful sight
By yon solemn river side,
Beneath the cloud of night.
There where through vapours dark
Strange forms I seem'd to see,
And nothing on either bank
Was what it seem'd to be.

" It was not a scathed willow
Beside the voiceless flood—
That dark shape watching the billow
Clad in a monkish hood,
Nought human was there inclining—
For I saw the moonbeam pale
Athwart the outline shining
As through a misty veil.

" In the silent river
A hand I saw it lave,

Seeking ever and ever
Something on the wave—
That ghostly hand was feeling,
Searching still in vain,
And the word came faintly stealing:
'She comes not back again.'"

The hermit bent in silence
Attentive to my tale—
And there passed a shade of sadness
Across his visage pale—
Yet from that sombre sadness
A faint light gleam'd awhile,
Though nought akin to gladness
Was in that transient smile.

"And thou, my son," he cried,
"That phantom too could'st see,
Kenn'd by the silent tide
Ere now of none but me!
Of heaven's mystic ways
A token I can read—

List then beside the kindling blaze,
Whilst I recount of other days,
A strange and piteous deed.

Not many years have bow'd my head,
Not age has blanch'd my brow,
For lustres five have scarcely fled,
Since I roam'd the world with as light a tread,
And with heart as light as thine.

I wore as thou my spurs of gold,
And my tresses of golden hair—
And though but twenty summers old
Was nor unknown among the bold,
Nor unheeded of the fair.

That happy past is now a dream,
Is a star in the milky plain.
It lends alone a pallid gleam,
But of youthful hope the kindling beam
Can warm me ne'er again.

One brother sole, of all our race,
Was left my love to claim
Alike in form, alike in face,
In courage equal, and in grace,
We differ'd but by name.

But he was cast in sterner mould,
More rash, more prone to ire,
And yet his humour fierce and bold
One spirit bland and blest controll'd
And calm'd his angry fire.

For he woo'd and won a maiden fair,
Proudest and first of all—
My lot was with that noble pair
The charms of tranquil love to share
In the old ancestral Hall.

But now the Hosts of Christendom
The Pagan land invade,
And away across the salt sea foam
My brother has left his blissful home
To join the far crusade.

He left his Hilda sorrowing there
To stem the battle tide,
Nor ought avail'd of tear or prayer,
He left his dame and his infant heir;
He would no more abide.

Long in the fight with lofty mien
He led his followers on,
And ever where his crest was seen,
Where glanced his falchion bright and keen,
Heroic deeds were done.

Think not that I in peaceful hall
A life of pleasure led,
Whilst sounded thus the trumpet call,
And there before the Paynim wall
Our Christian warriors bled.

Nor idle was, or lance or brand,
I have seen lusty blows,
And oft have led a gallant band
Upon the frontiers of our land,
Against invading foes.

I too in joust and tourney gay
Have striven not in vain.
For I have known my part to play,
And with the brave in knightly fray
A victor's wreath to gain.

First saw I in like feat of arms,
Where I successful strove,
My Clara rich in modest charms,
Who fill'd my soul with sweet alarms,
And taught me how to love.

Her winning smile and noble mien
Inspired me in the fight,
Resistless made my falchion keen,
And she, of love and beauty queen,
Crown'd the victorious knight.

Henceforth I woo'd that peerless maid,
Nor vainly urg'd my plea,
Yet is awhile my bliss delayed,
Nor till returns the far crusade,
May we united be.

But sweetly now the moments glide,
Blest moments past recall;
For still I meet my destin'd bride
In forest glade, on mountain side,
In bower, and festive hall.

And oft she sought in her domain
The pensive Hilda fair.
And well they loved like sisters twain,
Sharing each other's joy and pain,
As sisters twain should share.

And the bright glance of Clara dear,
With sweet and magic spell,
Alone that pensive dame could cheer,
Who mourn'd the absence long and drear
Of the one she loved so well.

And Clara oft with noble grace
My ruder toils would share,
Would mingle in the dangerous chace,
At courteous tourney hold her place,
And knightly armour wear.

But time rolls by, the war is o'er,
The weary troops return,
They hail with joy the native shore,
They reach the wish'd for home once more,
That prize they well did earn.

Yet not return'd that noble chief,
Nor came his faithful train—
Nor tidings were could bring relief
To hearts that pined in doleful grief,
And hop'd long years in vain.

At length, since all must end below,
Are ended doubts and fears,
On Afric's shore, at length we know,
Our lord made captive by the foe,
Had sighed for two sad years.

As homeward o'er the bounding wave
He strove with scanty train,
A corsair seized that warrior brave,
To Tunis bore, and left a slave,
In dungeon and in chain.

Within our hearts these tidings move
Of joy, than anguish shed,
For we had wept him o'er and o'er,
Deeming that he on Paynim shore,
Was numbered with the dead.

Hope glows in Hilda's gentle breast
To meet her lord once more.
Her loving zeal will know not rest,
Or, of his ransom high possess'd,
She seek the Spanish shore.

And soon she seeks the Spanish strand,
The heavy ransom found,
Of vassals true a gallant band
Escort their lady lance in hand,
On holy mission bound.

My Clara, clad in glittering steel,
Will join that mission too.
Dissuasion mocks with friendly zeal,
And heedless of my fond appeal,
She gaily smiles adieu.

Me fate forbade with cruel spite
To join the cavalcade,
For I to aid a brother knight
In an impending border fight,
A compact firm had made.

But hope is in my Clara's heart
Her smile has promise too,
Yet see I tears unbidden start
As, whilst we there in silent part,
She gaily smiles adieu.

I smil'd—but faintly smil'd again,
My heart was bleeding sore.
Then onward pass'd that joyous train,
I saw them skirt the distant plain,
I saw them never more.

— — —

But let me now with rapid pace,
Traverse the piteous tale,

For as the doleful past I trace,
Emotions strong my words efface,
And heart is nigh to fail.

The Afric shore is left behind,
The ransom'd captive free,
And, wafted by a favouring wind,
Too slow for his impatient mind,
He is crossing the restless sea.

Winds or waves no pace can keep,
With wishes that homeward fly,
Yet soon he spies beyond the deep
A distant headland blue and steep
Piercing the paler sky.

Upon that point high pois'd in air
The broad expanse to view,
Stands day by day the Hilda fair,
Breathing ever a silent prayer
As she looks on the waters blue.

Now at this moment one and same
Hearts each are other greeting,
His sail she kens and the oriflamme,
He sees the rock where that noble dame
In breathless hope is waiting.

And now at length that hope is crown'd,
Deferr'd through long sad years.
And he stands again on Christian ground,
And there his Hilda fair has found,
Adorn'd with smiles and tears.

There Clara too, whose maiden grace
Is veiled in knightly gear,
Tends to the chief a frank embrace,
Deputed in a brother's place,
His welcome home to bear.

For she with innocent intent
Her tender sex would hide,
Till, home arrived, with new content
Our chief may learn the blest event,
Shall make her then my bride.

My brother marked her noble air
Beside his beauteous dame;
Her eye of blue, and raven hair,
And, as he mark'd, a look of care
Upon his features came.

But sombre care could never stay
Where stay'd my Clara bright.
She pass'd to all her humour gay,
As can one taper's gentle ray
Unnumber'd lamps ignite.

But joy is fading as the grass,
And goes as all things go.
Some fleeting hours of gladness pass,
The last bright days that hence, alas,
My brother e'er must know.

By durance long, and want and woe,
His health robust was tried.
And now a fever, dull and slow,
Within his frame begins to glow,
Awhile he there must bide.

Abide awhile on couch of pain
Beside the Spanish shore,
By healing arts his health to gain,
Ere he can bear his arms again
In vigour as before.

And well each healing art was tried
By those who held him dear,
And each in turn the couch beside,
With anxious zeal his need supplied,
And smil'd his heart to cheer.

There is beside a river bright
A garden cool and green,
Where orange boughs with blossoms white,
And myrtles sweet embalm the night
And form a grateful skreen.

Here breaks the blue sea's murmuring wave
With ne'er receding sound.
And, moor'd within a mossy cave,
Where sea and stream united lave,
A little skiff is found.

Thither would sometimes Clara stray
Beside the waters clear,
Quitting awhile her humour gay,
To think of one was far away,
And drop a single tear.

One evening to her favorite spot
More sad than wont she stray'd,
And Hilda sought but spied her not,
Till there within the moss clad grot,
She found the pensive maid.

To float upon that tranquil stream
The skiff she had unbound,
For she, beneath the cold moonbeam,
Of me, her absent love would dream,
In musing thought profound.

Oft heaven in ways of mystery
Misfortune will foreshow.
This gloom, unknown, or whence or why,
On Clara's soul's yet cloudless sky,
Spoke of impending woe.

Hilda had mark'd her pensive mien,
More pensive still and sad,
And from such mood her friend would wean,
And lead her to the social scene
Her presence aye could glad.

And well she urged with accent bland,
Well urged with fond caress,
As by the little skiff they stand,
Pressing closely hand to hand
With sister tenderness.

What is it steals through cypress gloom
And past the myrtle shade
Then stands like ghost from yawning tomb,
Pale herald of some dismal doom,
In ghastly white array'd?

The chief whose rest wild visions chase
Has miss'd his Hilda fair,
Strange doubts his sickly mind embrace,
He has follow'd her track with stealthy pace,
And has found that loving pair.

And he hears the tones of Hilda bland,
And he sees the fond caress,
As by the little skiff they stand,
Pressing closely hand to hand
With sister tenderness.

Ah woe! Scarce will my failing breath
The sequel dire unfold—
But ne'er before were done to death
Fond hearts so innocent beneath
The moonbeam pure and cold.

There is beside a river bright
A garden cool and green,
And there two marble crosses white,
Of myrtles that embalm the night
Gleam forth from leafy skreen.

There sleep our loves, whilst mourns the wave
With ne'er receding sound
Near where within a mossy cave
Which sea and stream united lave
The little skiff was found.

I waited long my love's return,
I waited long in vain.—
And a horse and his rider at last discern
With frantic speed as the soil they spurn,
Coming over the distant plain.

And he came, that rider, wan and worn,
Devour'd by anguish keen.—
Sure never set eve nor rose the morn,
On one so reft, one so forlorn,
Since morn and eve have been.

And I learn how of these victims twain
Was Clara first who died.
And, dying, Hilda had told, ah vain!
How that sweet maid, thus madly slain,
Was my affianced bride.

That chief's despair, oh! who can tell?
That bitterness who could dream?
Commenced for him a pang of hell,
That crimson stain as pure it fell
Upon the limpid stream.

THE PARDON.

But pardon mortals all must crave,
And vengeance leave to Heaven.
My heart was buried in Clara's grave,
So I that despairing soul forgave
As I hoped to be forgiven.

He has left his hall and his wide domain,
He has quitted his arms for ever—
And he seeks, with wild and tortured brain,
This dreary spot, to still remain
By the side of the silent river.

For he said he saw his Hilda fair
As he wander'd I knew not whither,
He said, she ever was pointing there,
As on we roam'd I knew not where,
Until we wander'd hither.

For here she had bid him pardon gain,
Or pardon'd he would be never.

And *then* would be wash'd out the stain
When he should see her blood again
Upon this silent river.

So here, by doleful fortune borne,
I fixed our lonely dwelling.
And I pray'd for that poor soul forlorn
From fading eve till early morn,
My beads unwearied telling.

But never here would he abide,
Availed persuasion never.
He quits no more the water side,
Seeks blood—*her* blood upon the tide,
Of the still unsullied river.

And he died beside the rolling flood,
And I buried him by the willow,
In his mantle gray and monkish hood,
And to pray his grace and ghostly good
I have known nor rest nor pillow.

And still, my son, I here must bide,
Thus interceding ever,
Whilst he, still by the water's side,
Seeks vainly blood upon the tide.
Of the still unsullied river.

For as the billow fleeting by
Returns not from the main—
As float not back the winds that fly—
Nor bloom again the flowers that die—
Her blood comes not again.

The final word is spoken
Of the hermit's doleful tale.
And in silence long unbroken,
I watch his visage pale,
Bodings—vague—mysterious
My senses captive take.
And with impulse—strong—imperious
The silence thus I break.

You have told me of the knight—
You have told of Hilda fair—
Of the phantom of the night—
And what he is seeking there.
But father, nothing hast thou told
Of the son, the infant heir—
I pray thee then the fate unfold
Of the child of Hilda fair!

When I abandon'd arms and fame,
My brother's fate to share,
Not heedless was I of the name
That child should one day bear.
Within a cloister's sure retreat
I found him fitting place
Where he should gentle nurture meet
As best became his race.

For him the hall and wide domain
Were placed in trusty care.
That when he should his spurs attain,
He might bring honour there.

THE PARDON.

That he in tourney and in fight
His father's blade should wield,
And with new blazon make more bright
The glories of his shield.

But from that convent's walls he fled.
One sad ill-fated day.
And be he living yet or dead
My son I cannot say.
He fled to join some far campaign,
Or seek some foreign shore,
And heirless now is the domain
Of Karl de Waldebour.

———

He gazed in mute amaze
Upon the hermit pale,
As by the flickering blaze
Ended that piteous tale.
His tongue refused its aid,
Till at last he trembling cried,
" Then 'twas my father's shade
I saw by the sullen tide.

"That form that in the river
Its fingers seem'd to lave,
Something ever and ever
Seeking upon the wave.
And 'twas my mother's blood
He was seeking there in vain
When I came on the rolling flood
The child of Hilda slain!"

"Oh yes," the hermit cries,
"Thou art child of Hilda fair!
Those are her gentle eyes
And her tresses of golden hair.
Then shall he Heaven's mercy share,
And be free'd from his doleful pain
For *thou*, the blood of his Hilda fair,
Hast come back on the wave again."

There is within a tangled dell
A ruin void and lone.
The hermit pale has left his cell,
And his crucifix of stone.

THE PARDON.

The glittering casque he wore of old
Again his white locks wear
And in joust or fight, he joins a knight
With tresses of golden hair.

There's a silent river flowing
Mid evening vapours dank
And a beauteous flower is growing
Upon an ozier bank.
And there the moonbeam sleeps,
Like a smile from gracious heaven,
That whispers one who weeps
" His crime has been forgiven."

And there's a scathed willow
Beside the water's brim,
Into the voiceless billow
That droops a shatter'd limb.
You would say, ere nearer borne
On the untiring flood,
'Twas a figure aged and worn
And clad in a monkish hood.

Fragment of an Old Ballad.

WHITE owl sate on the castle wall
 Ring, ring, the chimes are gone,
A white owl sate on the castle wall,
 I toll'd three tolls, and he came at the call
  And the old Bell of Beaujey.

A feather will fly, and a wind will blow,
Ring, ring, the chimes are gone,
 The feather is gone where feathers do go,
But the lightest of all is a maid I know
 And the Old Bell of Beaujey.

FRAGMENT OF AN OLD BALLAD.

The moon shone over a field of ice,
    Ring, ring, the chimes are gone,
The old man counted his rats and mice,
    He told them false, so he told them twice,
        And the Old Bell of Beaujey.

The Bell of Beaujey.

THOU hast heard it once—hast heard it twice—
  To night, and yesterday.
Guard thee well to hear it thrice,
  Wander far away.
For never he 'scap'd death or dole
  Who heard three times the solemn toll
    Of the Bell of Beaujey.

And twice beside the dark wood
  Thou hast seen a dainty dame—
Twice out of the dark wood
  That dainty lady came—
But ever he had cause to wail
  Who met three times the spectre pale
    Of the Bell of Beaujey.

THE BELL OF BEAUJEY.

Long time at eve the solemn knell
    Has sounded ever,
But *who* that rang, and *where* the bell
    Known was never.
And at its summons no one came
    But from the wood the dainty dame
        To the Bell Tower of Beaujey.

He perished alone—day by day
    Amid ill gotten gain,
None knew the place—none knew the way,
    None knew how he toll'd in vain.
None knew but she, and she was dead,
    Slain by him she thought to wed,
        Who tolls the Bell of Beaujey.

Down, down beneath foundations deep,
    There it was he died.
Where rats and mice their revels keep,
    Nor living thing beside.
There still he tolls his own death knell
    Ever upon the unseen bell,
        The lost Bell of Beaujey.

A white owl sate on the castle wall
    In the moonlight cold,
And only he would come to the call
    As thrice it toll'd,
None other fowl—but he the owl,
    And the spectre pale of the lady frail
        To the Bell of Beaujey.

And thou hast heard it once and twice.
    Now and yesterday,
Tell thy beads—nor listen thrice,
    Wander far away,
For never he 'scap'd death or dole
    Who heard three times the solemn toll
        Of the Bell of Beaujey.

Where, where art thou.

WHERE, where art thou? I ask the mountain green
  The last repose of eve's expiring light—
I ask the phantoms of the chill ravine—
  And that dull flood where terror lurks at night—
Each place mysterious—and every where—
  And ever more—at morn and evening tide,
Oh silent witnesses of my despair
  I ask you ever—" Give me back my bride."

But vale and mountain and mysterious cave
Permit me not thy vanish'd form to see—
The savage solitude—the frightful wave
Hides thee for ever, lost to only me!
Vain to the summer light winds as they fly
So bland and joyous do I still complain,
All things are smiling, but not heed my cry
And summer breezes bring thee not again!

Where, where art thou? I ask the dewy glade
Through which we roam'd and smil'd in bygone years—
I ask the thicket with its dismal shade
Where I have seen thee weep—and shar'd thy tears—
I ask the sun—the sky—the earth—the moon—
All things—and ever more—at every tide—
Of life—of death—heaven—hell—I ask the boon,
I ask thee ever—" Give me back my bride."

But thicket dense—and dark and dewy dell—
Permit me not thy vanished form to see—
Sun—sky—earth—moon—life—death—and heaven—and hell—
Hide thee for ever, lost to only me.

Vain to the summer light winds as they fly
So bland and joyous, do I still complain—
Alive or dead all smile—but mock my cry—
And summer breezes bring thee not again!

FINIS.

LONDON:
Printed by A. Schulze, 13, Poland Street.

www.ingramcontent.com/pod-product-compliance
Lightning Source LLC
Chambersburg PA
CBHW030410170426
43202CB00010B/1560